MT. HOOD COMMUNITY COLLEGE
TUTORIAL

HOW TO MASTER TEST TAKING

MT. HOOD COMMUNITY COLLEGE

TUTORIAL

HOW TO MASTER TEST TAKING

FRED A ANDERSON

SKILLS IMPROVEMENT
P.O. BOX 595
AURORA, CO 80040

To my wife, Hannelore,
my mother and father
for their sustaining
inspiration through the years.

FIRST EDITION

HOW TO MASTER TEST TAKING

EDITED BY HANNELORE ANDERSON

Copyright © 1981 by Fred A. Anderson.
All rights reserved. No part of this
publication may be reproduced by
any means, without prior written
permission of the publisher, except for
brief excerpts used in newspaper or
magazine reviews.

LIBRARY OF CONGRESS CATALOG
CARD NUMBER 81-90062

INTERNATIONAL STANDARD BOOK NUMBER
0-939570-00-9

PRINTED IN THE UNITED STATES OF AMERICA

PREFACE

Let me introduce myself: I'm Fred A. Anderson, your author. One of my primary purposes in writing this book is to share with you, all the test-taking skills I've acquired over the past ten years. I originally became interested in test taking because of a desire to achieve a higher promotion test score. After discovering one test-taking skills book in the library, I searched for more. Eventually I obtained a number of books and articles on the subject. I applied the techniques I'd learned and did improve my score.

Later, I applied these skills to college-level exams (CLEP) and received my first degree with the minimum number of required resident courses (five). Once I started, I couldn't stop. I've taken over seventy-five college examinations with a pass-rate of over 80% (without knowing almost ANYTHING about the subjects I tested in). The results of my efforts are a B.S. degree from the University of the State of New York, an A.A. degree from the University of Maryland, and two A.A.S. degrees from the Community College of the Air Force (CCAF). I'm within one course of a third A.A.S. degree from City Colleges of Chicago and plan to finish my M.A. degree within the next two years. I know that test-taking skills work, because I satisfied all requirements for my B.S. degree with only five classroom courses!

For approximately three years I taught test-taking skills at the U. S. Air Forces in Europe NCO Academy. Presently I'm teaching test-taking skills at the Metropolitan Technical Community College in Omaha, Nebraska. As you can see, I've benefited tremendously from test-taking skills, and you can too.

I wish to express my sincere thanks to the individuals who helped with this edition. My wife, Hannelore, contributed substantially to its clarity and continuity. The book cover, logo design and graphics were artistically created by my brother, Fresno. I'm particularly grateful for the editing assistance given by the Metropolitan Technical Community College staff: Ruth Iliff, coordinator, and the IDEA Program instructors, Janet Blimling, Jeanne Cork, Cathy Harlow, D'Arla Skinner and Vicki Weil. I'm also grateful to Prentice-Hall and Field Enterprises for granting copyright permissions.

INTRODUCTION

You're reading this book because you have a sincere desire to improve your test scores. With that in mind, I've packed it with hundreds of tips, hints and techniques to help you raise exam scores to the highest possible level. But first, let's discuss our test oriented society.

We were introduced to our first test with the breath-of-life test given at birth, and our final examination will be the test of vital signs at death. Between these extremes, we take thousands of tests that will control our lives and shape our careers. Collectively, exams do make or break us. They determine our successes and failures.

At Columbia University, research was conducted to determine what constitutes success. They discovered that success was made up of three main ingredients. To be considered successful by your standards, and by others, three elements are essential: skill, knowledge and attitude. Not being satisfied with just identifying these factors, they sought to determine the relative importance of each. The results of their research was that attitude make up 93% of success! Skill and knowledge were responsible for only 7%. An amazing fact.

We've always been led to believe that skill and knowledge were significant in achieving any degree of success. Columbia's research proved that wrong. Verify this research personally: recall some past, unpleasant task or project you were involved in. You had sufficient knowledge and skill to accomplish it, but you had a negative attitude concerning it. The job was eventually completed, but you had difficulty finishing it. Contrast that with this situation: recall another past task you performed with little or no skill or knowledge, but a positive attitude. Your positive attitude more than made up for your lack of skill and knowledge. Not only did you complete it with fewer problems, you also experienced a wonderful

vii

feeling of accomplishment.

Don't underestimate the value of attitude. With the proper attitude you can do almost anything. Apply that positive, confident attitude to test taking. Read this book with the positive attitude that you CAN improve your test-taking abilities. Have confidence in yourself and in this book to help you achieve this goal. Remember, attitude is everything! (93%)

Another misconception many people have is that a person cannot be taught to improve their test-taking skills. Stop and think about this. Courses are available to teach us counseling skills, to train us to read better, and achieve proficiency in thousands of other subjects. Why are testing skills so different? They aren't. Test taking is an art that can be taught. An effective program of instruction and practice will improve your testing skills, if you apply them. We all know that nothing will take the place of knowledge of the subject. But that's not enough. Understanding the subject will never guarantee success. No matter how long you study for a test, there will be questions that you can't answer. That's where this book comes in. It contains those principles, techniques and strategies that will enable you to conquer those questions you either don't know, or are not sure of. Read this book, study it, apply the skills, and you'll be a master test taker.

> All of us have two educations;
> one which we receive from others;
> another and the most valuable,
> which we give ourselves.
> ---John Randolph

I believe your future test scores should reflect your complete knowledge of the subject. I define complete knowledge as absolute knowledge, plus partial knowledge. Your absolute knowledge is the informtion you positively know, without a doubt. Partial knowledge is those things you know something about, but it's incomplete. Example: you know some things concerning the operating and constructing of a car. But you don't know enough to explain its principle of operation in detail or to repair it. In my opinion, your partial knowledge is thousands of times more than your absolute knowledge. You simply aren't aware of how much partial knowledge you've acquired over the years. You've accumulated this tremendous amount of knowledge through everyday living: TV, radio, newspapers, books, interests and hobbies. I challenge you to put it to use where it counts--during a test.

Over the years I've read many books and articles on test taking. Although most of them were helpful, all had the same fault--they were incomplete. They didn't take the reader through the entire test-taking process. Also, many filled their pages with unneeded information for the average test taker. I felt there was a need for a practical test-taking guide, with only that information needed to prepare for, take and review tests. I've attempted to get to the point, stay on the subject, and make every written word count. Your time is valuable and I respect that. I've kept it short: in words, but not in information.

Along with its briefness, I've also tried to keep it simple. The strategies in chapter 6 go from simple to complex. Because of that, some of the later ones you may have to read more than once to fully comprehend the principle and logic behind them. But considering their complexity, I've kept the explanation as direct and uncomplicated as possible.

The example questions used were selected because of their uncommonness. The less you can relate to the content of the question, the better. This approach will motivate you to use the strategies, rather than use your subject knowledge or experience to determine the answers. Now it's time for you to start--Good Luck!

TEST PRAYER

Now I lay me down to study
I pray the Lord I won't go nutty,
If I should fail to learn this junk,
I pray the Lord I will not flunk.
But if I do, don't pity me at all,
Just lay my bones down in the
   study hall;
Tell my teacher I did my best,
Then pile my books upon my
   chest.
Now I lay me down to rest
And pray I'll pass tomorrow's
   test.
If I should die before I wake,
That's one less test I'll have to
   take.

---

*From the "Ann Landers" column, ©1978 by Field Enterprises, Inc., Chicago, Illinois, 60611: Appearing in the European Stars and Stripes Newspaper. Reproduced by permission.

CONTENTS

1. PREPARING FOR THE TEST

    Weeks before   1
    Postpone if   2
    Days before   2
    Tools of your trade   3
    The day before   3

2. ESSENTIAL TEST-TAKING PRINCIPLES

    Test phraseology   5
    Methods of answer selection   6
    General guidelines   7
    Most correct answer   9
    Easy questions first   10
    Time considerations   11
    When to guess   13
    Changing answers   15
    Scratch paper   15
    Test success   16

3. DAY OF THE TEST

    Plan you morning   19
    Arrival   19
    Selecting the best seat   20
    Pre-test activities   20

4. WITH TEST IN HAND

    Test directions   23
    Scanning the test   24
    Your starting point   24
    Read questions carefully   25

5. KEY WORDS AND PHRASES

    Abolutes   27
    Qualifiers   28
    Determiners   29
    Foreign and strange words   29
    Key word percentages   30

6. EXAMINATION STRATEGIES

    Frequency of occurrence 31
    Longest answer 32
    A/An connection 33
    Root and prefix clues 34
    Physical position 34
    Negative questions 35
    Question and answer association 35
    Related question disclosure 36
    All of the above 38
    None of the above 39
    Relative position 40
    Nonparallel options 41
    Double negatives 42
    "X" substitution 42
    Judgment questions 43
    Deceptive computation 44
    Complex questions 45
    Inconsistent form 47
    Similar choices 48
    Opposite choices 49
    Overlapping alternatives 50

7. AFTER THE EASY QUESTIONS

    Now the hard questions 51
    Compute your "rough" score 52
    A response for every question 52
    Check for mismarks 53
    Determine test composition 53

8. AFTER THE TEST

    Test review 55
    Afterthoughts 56

    BIBLIOGRAPHY 57

1

PREPARING FOR THE TEST

WEEKS BEFORE

The best approach for you, the test taker, is to start preparing weeks before the testing date. There is no substitute for knowledge of the subject matter. Regular and consistent study of the exam subject is a must. With all the skills and techniques mentioned here, if you fail to study and review during the final weeks prior to an examination, you're destined to achieve a lower score than if you prepared properly.

Set up a study schedule and stick to it. It should be at approximately the same time each day and preferably at the same location. Select a quiet place as far away from distractions as possible. Studying with the TV, radio or stereo within hearing distance, isn't the best learning environment. Also, try to locate your study area away from playing children, barking dogs and traffic, or any other similar distractions, that prevent you from complete concentration.

Along with your intellectual preparation, don't forget your body. It also needs exercise: of a different nature, but just as important as your mind. It's hard to have an alert mind with a sluggish body. Being physically unfit prevents you from studying effectively, and will, on test day, affect your test performance. Engage in some form of physical exercise daily. Don't overdo it to the point you're exhausted, but to a sufficient degree to keep your body tuned up, both physically and mentally. A well planned and executed program is the best confidence builder you can have.

POSTPONE IF

Some adverse event or situation may occur during the weeks before your testing date that prompts you to attempt to postpone or reschedule your testing date or time. To avoid any misinterpretation, I'm only suggesting you request a delay if you feel you have a legitimate reason for doing so. The individuals controlling the test schedule will ultimately decide whether your reason is legitimate.

Besides being ill or sick, there are other reasons many people consider valid. I'm an evening person: meaning, I function better mentally in the afternoon and evening. If I have a choice of taking an exam in the morning or afternoon, I'll schedule it in the afternoon. Followers of biorhythms feel that when their intellectual curve is at rock bottom, it's a justifiable reason to seek another testing date. If you're into horoscopes and your astrological sign indicates something less than optimum on test day, you might consider asking for a more advantageous day. For women, an additional factor can affect your exam score. Several studies concluded that just before or during the menstrual cycle, test performance suffers. So, if you have in the past experienced this, I strongly recommend getting your test day changed, if possible. Realistically, however, in many testing situations, a postponement or change in date or time isn't likely. But you'll never know until you try.

DAYS BEFORE

Now that the time is almost here, a complete

review of the test-taking skills you've learned and perfected is in order. If you haven't started already, get a highlighter or a pen to underline important words, phrases and sentences as you read this book. It can save a tremendous amount of time during subsequent readings. I'm never without a highlighter when I'm reading. Once I've underlined or highlighted important points, I can review the book at a later date in less than one-tenth the time it took me to read it originally. It's possible to do this by reading only the highlighted areas and skimming the rest. After you've adequately reexamined the test-taking skills, continue studying and reviewing the subject you'll soon be tested on. Physical activity should be continued also, to maintain your total body at its peak effiency.

TOOLS OF YOUR TRADE

Most test takers overlook some of the mechanics of being prepared on test day. You probably wouldn't consider attending classes without at least a pencil, paper and textbook. But without thinking, all of us have arrived to test not having the essential tools. Things I consider important enough to collect the night before are: pencils, pens, watch, cassette recorder, tapes, and study reference material. Insure the batteries in your recorder are fresh or fully charged up (if you use the rechargeable type). A slide rule, protractor, calculator may be on your list of needed items, if so, assemble them in one place and check them over the night before. Your need for the majority of these items should be clear, and I'll explain the purpose and use of the less-obvious items in chapter 8. Don't leave home without them, although only a few of your testing tools will be with you in the examination room.

THE DAY BEFORE

How you spend this day will affect your exam score more than most persons realize. The key is to control and regulate your emotional state and physical activity. Make the day before your test a calm and relaxing one. Even if you have to take a day off from work, or take a day of vacation or leave, it's well worth it. If you work under pressure or in a demanding job, a day away from the office is the only way to insure a calm day before testing. I routinely take the day off before an important exam. Avoid all conflicts and disturbances: simply put them off or delay them until after the exam. Follow your normal routine, with one exception, don't study or cram. If you've been studying up to now, you know as much as you'll learn before tomorrow. Cramming the last minute won't do any good the day before your test. Involve yourself in some activity. In other words, do something to take your mind off the test. I always have something to do around the house, or a neglected hobby or interest to catch up on. Just keep your mental and physical activity "light." You don't need a backache or dull mind tomorrow.

This is also the day to gather up your tools. A beneficial way to spend this evening before the test is to relax--your way, watching TV, going to a movie or whatever turns you on. Once again, keep it light, nothing heavy. End the day early: go to bed a little earlier than normal, without drugs. A good night's rest will keep you awake while reading question number 38 tomorrow.

The coming chapter departs from the sequence of events leading up to your testing day. I feel it's important for you to be fully aware of fundamental test-taking principles at this stage of your test preparation.

2

ESSENTIAL TEST-TAKING PRINCIPLES

TEST PHRASEOLOGY

Knowing the terms used in testing will aid you in grasping and understanding the testing business. More specifically, being familiar with these phrases will enable you to comprehend much more of what follows in this book. Eventhough most of this may be familiar to you, let's start with the basics.

The smallest composite unit of a test is the question, or as some know it, the test item. It is composed of two parts, the stem and the alternatives. The stem is the statement, or question, that poses a problem for you to answer. It could be a complete sentence, an incomplete statement or a question. The alternatives of a question are those three, four or five words, phrases or statements, that you select from to answer the question correctly. Alternatives are also called options, choices and responses. They are usually labeled A, B, C, D: or 1, 2, 3, 4. The alternatives are further broken down into distractors and the correct choice or keyed response. That's where this book will help you: selecting the right alternative from the distractors, to correctly answer the question statement in the stem.

Collectively, the questions make up the test. Tests are categorized in numerous ways. There are objective tests (multiple-choice, matching and true-false) as contrasted with subjective tests (fill-in, completion and essay). Another way to compare tests is by the degree of emphasis placed on testing time. That's basically the difference between speed and power tests. A speed test is designed, so that most test takers won't finish in the time limit. But, most of the exams you'll be taking, will be of the power test class. This type provides sufficient time to permit completion by the vast majority of testers.

Then, there is yet another break-out: the teacher-made test (nonstandardized) and the standardized test. We've all taken teacher-made tests in school, so no further explanation is needed. The standardized test is what we now take for job placement, advancement, promotion, etc. Almost all standardized tests are prepared by subject-matter experts and test psychologists. For that reason, you won't find as many clues in them. Nevertheless, there are enough clues, some unavoidable, to make it worth developing your test taking skills.

METHODS OF ANSWER SELECTION

The individual questions cannot all be approached in the same manner, if you expect to get the majority correct. The various methods are:

1. RECALL OF KNOWLEDGE is the best manner to arrive at the answer. After reading the question, you know the answer and locate it among the alternatives. Some questions can be answered without much thought. However, no matter how much we study and prepare for a test, there will be questions we just aren't sure of.

The remaining methods identify six other approaches employed to answer test items.

2. COMPUTATION is used when mathematics is required to determine the keyed response. You'll need this skill on math, electronics and other technical questions.

3. LIMITED ASSOCIATION is helpful when confronted with matching-type questions and some multiple-choice items. By associating the elements of these types of questions, the answer can be determined.

4. PROCESS OF ELIMINATION or deduction is one of my primary approaches on test items. By eliminating some of the distractors, I'm left with, at best, the answer; and if that isn't possible, at least I've narrowed the choices down to two or three. This is the key skill in getting you through those difficult questions.

5. TEST CONSTRUCTION CLUES, addressed later under "TECHNIQUES AND STRATEGIES," are those subtle clues that all tests contain. A knowledge of what to look for is invaluable to the test taker.

6. THE EDUCATED OR REASONED GUESS is what has been called a calculated guess or strong hunch. This valid test-taking technique enables you to receive credit for your partial knowledge, along with your absolute knowledge. The combination of these two make up your complete knowledge. An unskilled test taker usually fails to receive a true test score, simply because she or he doesn't guess.

7. AN UNQUALIFIED GUESS is unquestionably the last resort. Because of that, most individuals shun this approach; but I say use it when all else fails. There is only one type of question experts say you shouldn't guess at. The situation is mentioned later in this chapter. When you're confronted with the choice of guessing or leaving the question unanswered, go ahead and guess.

GENERAL GUIDELINES

Many small and seemingly minor considerations add up to a successful testing session. Some very general techniques follow. Collectively, they give you a sizable edge on the unskilled tester. That advantage will be reflected in your score. Exam panic or test anxiety can really hurt you on test day. Up to a point, some tenseness is beneficial and will help you achieve a high degree of alertness, but excessive worry puts you in a state of panic. Panic in true emergency situations enables you to perform physical feats beyond your normal capacity; but mental ability is what you need in this situation, and extreme anxiety only drains your mind to the point of confusion. Controlling it to an acceptable degree will permit you to approach each question with a clear, functioning mind.

As for teacher-made tests, it's wise to remember that most teachers aren't trained to construct tests. But don't look for trick questions on any exam. Most test makers won't resort to this sneaky approach. Also, don't read anything into the question. The words in the stem have been carefully chosen to precisely state the question. Remember, the answer you select must be entirely true for it to be correct. Your answer should be based on the study reference material, not your own experiences. The only exceptions are if the study material didn't cover that area, or you're asked general knowledge or judgment type questions.

Use common sense when thinking through each question, don't engage in tunnel vision. I've heard individuals comment after a test, "I knew which answer they wanted, but I didn't agree, so I marked the way I thought was best." Then these individuals wonder why they don't score high or get promoted. Try to put yourself in the test maker's shoes, then answer accordingly.

If you encounter an outdated question, don't panic. The question may have been valid when the test was prepared, but due to a fast changing world, it's no longer correct. Use the test copyright or publication date to guide you in selecting the answer. The only time that this strategy may not apply is when the choices contain both the old correct response and the new correct response. Then just take a pick.

Selecting the response is one thing, but recording it on your answer sheet is another. Each response should be clear, heavy and distinct. Insure each mark is within the space provided and doesn't overrun it. Record answers in the correct space. To minimize any mismarks, check your responses every ten or fifteen questions. An out of sequence mark will make most of your subsequent responses incorrect. Don't doodle on either the answer sheet or test booklet. When erasing, make sure you completely remove every trace of lead. The above careless mistakes will cost you dearly.

Let me make one final note on marking your answer sheet. To effectively use every second, record your responses on the answer sheet after each question. Saving the recording chore until you've answered all questions can be disastrous, and it consumes valuable time.

MOST CORRECT ANSWER

A smart test taker selects the first correct answer spotted, however, the wise one chooses the most correct answer. As mentioned before, each question contains among its alternatives, the keyed response and a number of distractors. The distractors are selected to be plausible and acceptable to the misinformed test taker. Some distractors are either partially correct or common misconceptions, designed to appear attractive to the unskilled tester. A wise test taker, however, will view these distractors as erroneous, unsound, unreasonable, or too broad or too narrow to be the correct response. Each distractor you can eliminate increases your chances of getting that question right.

The correct answer will almost always contain some of the following characteristics. It will be the most encompassing and inclusive alternative of the group. It's usually the most general and qualified choice available. Because the keyed response contains the above traits, it's usually the longest response. Incorrect choices can be stated concisely and in fewer words. It usually takes more words to state something correctly. Your goal then is to select the BEST response of the available alternatives.

Limit your thinking to the stated options.

Don't try to interpret an alternative to mean some other possibility not given as an alternative. Select only from those given and nothing else. The above skills are to be used only if you can't determine the answer in any other way. If you know which alternative is correct, answer it and continue without further thought.

EASY QUESTIONS FIRST

Most test takers waste time by spending too much time on hard or difficult questions. You're working against yourself if you do this. During your next exam, try this technique. Carefully read the stem of the question and pick out the key words and phrases. Attempt to answer the question without looking at the alternatives. Then look at the choices to see if your anticipated answer is among them. If you find it, mark your answer sheet and go on to the next one. If not, read the complete question again; this time eliminating as many distractors as you can, and record the remaining possible answers on your scratch paper. Don't spend anymore time on this question. At this point, you've finished with the question, so go on to the next item. Erase any thoughts of the previous question from your mind. Your subconscious will take over and usually the next time you read it, you'll have enough added insight to select the answer. Concentrate on only one question at a time. Follow these steps throughout the test.

If, after reading a question twice, you can't determine the answer, eliminate as many distractors as possible. Record the possible choices on your scratch paper, and start on the next question. By following this sequence you can more than double your "apparent" time. I define apparent time as your subjective judgment of the passage of time, when you're not looking at a clock or watch. If you're one of those individuals who never has sufficient time to finish a test, this approach will give more than enough time to finish. Try it and see.

TIME CONSIDERATIONS

As I mentioned earlier, your most pressing concern during a test is time. Some individuals don't finish within the time limit, simply because of inefficient testing habits. I too suffered from those self-defeating habits, until I started using these more efficient approaches. Maintaining absolute control of my time during a test has been the greatest single factor in my testing success. I know it can work for you too.

The first concern is to determine how many minutes or seconds you have to answer each question. You should compute this as soon as you're aware of the time limit and the number of questions. You may sometimes have this information before the testing date, and at other times, not until you're handed the test. In either case, compute it as soon as you have it. Let's say you're taking a one-hundred question test and have one and one-half hours (ninety minutes) to complete it. By simple division, you determine you have less than one minute per question (9/10 of a minute). With this useful information, you must now pace yourself accordingly. Answer the easy questions first, as you won't need all the allotted time per question to answer them. Use the technique outlined in the previous section. Remember, after attempting to answer the difficult questions, eliminate identifiable distractors and record the remaining possible answers on scratch paper. Once you've finished the less difficult items, you'll have a considerable amount of extra time to devote to those more difficult ones.

Now, go through that list of unanswered questions and attempt again to answer them. Here is where your recording of the possible answers for each hard question will save even more time. If, for example, you found question 7 a sticky one, an unskilled person would only make a note of the question number and go back to it. But being the alert test taker you are, in addition to the number of the question, you also were able to identify and eliminate choices A and D as distractors. So next to the number 7 on your scratch paper, you put B and C, the remaining choices. When you return to question 7, you're only concerned with two alternatives, whereas the unskilled tester is again confronted with four. By initially eliminating one or two of the alternatives you spend less time reconsidering the remaining options. This is a tremendous time saver. It automatically takes less time to think through a reduced number of choices. Why should you have to reconsider ALL the options again, after you've already discarded some during the first attempt. I consider this technique to be the cornerstone of skillful testing.

Some other time factors should also be considered. Your test preview and test review times will also consume portions of the total time limit. However, if you follow the above steps in answering both the easy questions and the difficult ones, you'll have ample time to preview and review.

Your start time, mid-point time and stop time should be noted on the scratch paper. Record your start time, compute your stop time and record it. Now determine your mid-point time. It would be forty-five minutes after your start time in the previous example I used. The mid-point time is used to check your progress at the half-way point. You should be on question 51, forty-five minutes after the start time. But if you aren't, the half-way mark is the time to adjust your pace for the remainder of the test. If you happen to be on question 39 at the forty-five minute point, you now know you'll have to increase your pace for the remaining questions. Hopefully, you'll be past question 50, if so, continue at the same comfortable pace. The additional time can always be used at the end.

Since pace is time oriented, let's discuss it here. Work as rapidly as possible, but carefully, without sacrificing accuracy. During the testing session, try and take a break every half hour to clear your mind. This break should only be from forty-five to sixty seconds. Close your eyes, stretch your limbs and relax in the chair to rejuvenate yourself, mentally and physically. Practice being the last to leave the testing room.

Use all available time. Chapter 7 mentions the productive things you should engage in during the remaining minutes of the session. Follow these time guidelines and you'll conquer your worst test enemy, time.

WHEN TO GUESS

Always! Forget about everything you've heard before. Give yourself permission to guess when all other techniques fail. The odds are in your favor whenever you guess, with one minor exception. Before I address when not to guess, let me explain why I strongly encourage you to always guess.

There are two types of tests you may take. The first kind is a standard test without a scoring formula or any penalty for guessing. In other words, if you correctly answered eighty questions out of one hundred, your score would be 80. The number of questions you answered correctly is your final grade. Your wrong answers won't count against your score, they're just incorrect. This kind of exam can be identified when you read the test directions. It will encourage you to answer every question, or guess at questions. If the directions DO NOT contain a statement warning you "not to guess" or mention a scoring formula, you're taking this type of test. On this test, guess, guess, guess! What can you lose? The wrong answers can't affect your score. Without any knowledge of the questions you're guessing on, the law of averages says you'll answer one out of every four correctly. You have a 25% chance of getting each question right, assuming there are four alternatives. With five alterntive-questions, you still have a 20% chance of answering a question correctly. There is never ANY reason for not marking something down for each question on a test such as this. Yet some individuals continue to leave items unanswered. It doesn't make any sense.

Many of the tests you'll be taking will be of the scoring formula type. A test of this sort will penalize you for wrong answers. Don't let that stop you from guessing though, because you're still ahead, percentage-wise. This type of a test is also revealed in the test directions. They will either be worded to discourage you from guessing, contain a statement advising you of the penalty for guessing, or mention a scoring formula. These statements shouldn't affect your approach to this test. The statement is only informing you of the ground rules. This is how your final score is arrived at, on a score-corrected test.

I'll use the previous example. You positively knew the answers to eighty of the one hundred questions. After answering those, you guessed at the remaining twenty, and correctly answered eight. The remaining twelve questions you answered incorrectly. Your score before applying the scoring formula is 88. Your score will be adjusted by taking one correct answer away from the 88 for every three answers you missed. This reduces your score by four points, leaving you with a final score of 84. You've gained four points by guessing, as compared to just responding to only the questions you knew. This illustration was based on a test with four alternatives for each question. For test items containing five choices, one correct response is taken away from your raw score for every four wrong answers.

On an average, chance guessing will net you one correct out of four tries, and all the scoring formula does is to cancel out your chance-guess advantage. Even if you only chance guess, without using any of the skills and techniques, you haven't lost anything. $84 - 4 (12 \div 3) = 80$, you receive the same score you started with, if you only answered those questions you were very sure of. Now, add the numerous test-taking skills and your subject knowledge to your chance guess factor, and you'll surely answer more than one-fourth of the "guessed-at" questions correctly.

A scientific guide to follow if you're still cautious is: if you can eliminate or discard at least ONE of the alternatives, it is to your advantage to guess. This applies to all multiple-choice questions, regardless of the number of alternatives. Your final score on the next test you take will be higher if you eliminate at least one of the distractors and guess at the remaining alternatives. The facts have been given to you. Now it's up to you to apply them.

Statistically, the only time you shouldn't guess is when you can't eliminate any of the choices, and you're taking the type of test with a scoring correction formula. It is true that in this situation you don't have an advantage, but you're not at a disadvantage either. The odds are even. For that reason, I'll guess without hesitation. I have nothing to lose, and neither have you.

CHANGING ANSWERS

Some say it's OK, others say it shouldn't be done. I say the average test taker can improve their score by changing answers--if. The "if" is significant. "IF" YOU HAVE INDISPUTABLE EVIDENCE that the option you previously selected is wrong, then change it. Your proof must be undeniable and beyond reasonable doubt. A number of studies have indicated that scores usually improve when answers are changed. Some conditions I consider valid enough to change answers are: misreading the question originally, recall of information which had previously slipped your mind, the answer revealed elsewhere in the test, and a previous oversight of a relevant fact.

Never change an answer on a second hunch! First impressions are usually correct. A more individual approach to changing answers is to analyze the type of person you are. There are those who habitually change answers from right to wrong, and others who customarily change from wrong to right. You can verify which category you're in from returned tests. By now, you should be aware of your habits, and you may want to use this as a guide in future tests.

SCRATCH PAPER

Never be without scratch paper. It's the most important item other than your pencil, when you're taking any multiple-choice test. If you aren't issued paper, request it. I've never been denied it in a testing session. However, avoid bringing paper into the testing room. The test administrator may view this with suspicion. You don't need that. You may, however, on a rare occasion have to search for some, if the test proctor doesn't have any. Just obtain permission.

Let us discuss how to use the scratch paper. As soon as you are in the testing room and have paper available, start jotting down the formulas, dates, lists, names, devised acronyms and abbreviations you want to recall during the test. You've committed them to memory up to this time, so relieve your mind now, and put them on paper. It's much easier to read them during the test than to mentally recall them. You'll be under much pressure, so give yourself a break. There is nothing illegal or unethical in doing this, as long as you didn't bring them in the room with you recorded on something.

During the test, use the paper to jot down those hard questions, along with the remaining alternatives you selected for further consideration. If you can't recall this great time-saving technique, read the "EASY QUESTIONS FIRST" section again. Scratch paper is also needed to determine the composition of the test.

TEST SUCCESS

*A Cornell University investigator surveyed 240 high school students, who were high-scoring test takers. They were asked what suggestions they would give a new student unfamiliar with the school's tests. Their tips are rank-ordered:

---

*From the book, THE COMPLETE GUIDE TO TAKING TESTS, by Bernard Feder. ©1979 by Bernard Feder. Published by Prentice-Hall, Inc., Englewood Cliffs, New Jersey 07632. Reproduced by permission.

Read directions (or questions carefully)	44%
Don't spend too much time on one question	27%
Recheck your answers for errors	20%
Guess if you don't know the answers	18%
Eliminate possible foils and distractions	17%
Look for leads from other questions	13%
Answer easier questions first	8%
Plan your time	7%
Don't read into questions (or answers) too deeply	5%

    A group of college students thought that the two most important reasons for their high performance on tests were "test understanding" and "comprehension and reading ability." Interestingly enough, knowledge of subject matter was NOT usually listed among the top reasons given by any of the studies in which students themselves were asked about test success.

    I consider this chapter critical to test success. Become very familiar with these principles. Review them before each test. Knowing and applying these basic guidelines will do more for you on test day than all the strategies combined. Let's resume the test preparation sequence on the morning of the test.

3
DAY OF THE TEST

PLAN YOUR MORNING

Last night you retired earlier than normal, therefore this morning you shouldn't have any difficulty getting up a few minutes earlier. Set your alarm clock to insure this. It's important to follow your daily morning routine and to resist the urge to cram. Have a "test morning" breakfast which should be sustaining, containing proteins and light sweets. Stay away from fats and starches, as much as possible.

A physical and mental warm up is helpful. Light exercise before a bath or shower will relieve some of the effects of sitting during the test. A quick review of concepts, generalizations, key points and formulas will start those brain cells functioning. Gather up and take your testing materials with you as you depart home earlier than normal. Being late for a test is a demoralizing and embarrassing experience. Don't cancel out all your planning and preparation with a late start.

ARRIVAL

Arrive early, but not too early. When there

is too much time before a test, people tend to converse and discuss the test and their apprehensions. Avoid these groups; their conversations will usually increase your anxiety level and confuse you unnecessarily. Before you enter the testing room, satisfy your physical needs, go to the restroom, get a drink of water or have that last smoke.

SELECTING THE BEST SEAT

Front row center! That's where it's at. Seat selection is critical to your concentration and comfort. The better seats are in the front of the room. The less distractions (people, furniture, pictures, and windows) between you and the test administrator, the better. Friends and attractive individuals will also distract you at the very time you need full concentration.

As for the comfort aspects, pick a seat away from the window. Drafts and glare will hinder your performance. Sit where you'll have proper lighting and adequate ventilation. If there are different types of chairs in the room, select the most comfortable one, even if it means moving it to your preferred location.

PRE-TEST ACTIVITIES

Once you're settled in the seat, stay there. Your remaining time before the test should be spent in pre-test activities. Pay no attention to others. Your first concern is to write down those lists, formulas, key ideas, acronyms, etc., you've memorized for the test. The procedure for securing paper was discussed in the "SCRATCH PAPER" section. Once you've relieved your mind of that burden, it's time to relax your body and mind.

As mentioned before, a limited degree of stress and tension is healthy. Beyond that point they're detrimental. A few simple exercises will enable you to achieve the desired level of relaxation and calm before the exam. First, loosen your tie, belt, shoe laces and other restricting articles. Slow down your breathing and breathe deeper than normal. Close your eyes and go through a relaxation sequence. If you're not familiar with this, read one of the many books on relaxation. A typical relaxation sequence involves alternately tensing and relaxing muscles in limbs and other parts of your body in separate steps. Engage in this activity until you're either almost in twilight consciousness, or the test administrator jolts you out of it for the start of the test. If the former occurs first, slowly regain complete consciousness. You will now be free of excessive tension and stress.

This is the best time to become familiar with your provided testing materials, if they're available. Look at your answer sheet or card. Develop a working knowledge of its layout, format and the location of the response areas. After you start the test is the worst time to try and figure it out. Glance at the test booklet covers. You may discover a mistake. A wrong or outdated test error is best corrected before the exam starts. If there is any remaining time, use it to mentally review your test-taking skills. Also keep in mind, a skilled test taker, such as you, can increase scores from 10 to 20%. Good luck.

4

WITH TEST IN HAND

TEST DIRECTIONS

    Reading and understanding test directions are critical. Don't underestimate their importance. I was guilty of not reading the directions, and did it cost me! In the early 1970's I took a promotion test. Individuals in my occupation were given an older edition of the current test, while all others used the current edition. The test administrator read the directions aloud, using the new edition. I assumed that everyone had the same test and listened intently to him without following his delivery in my own booklet. My older edition allowed a longer completion time than the edition the others had. I took the test, and later that day discovered from a co-worker that I should've received additional time. I verified this, submitted a written protest, and it was eventually acted on at the highest level of the organization. They stated that although I'd been denied sufficient testing time, it would be an injustice to the other individuals if I was allowed to retake the test. Don't let that happen to you.

    Read along CAREFULLY, as the test proctor reads the directions aloud. If you have any questions, ask. Don't hesitate--your score will affect your career and life. The same applies to directions for each part of a test. The test maker wouldn't put directions before each separate part if there wasn't a difference between the various sections. Take a hint and read them.

SCANNING THE TEST

You've just been told to start the test--the clock is running, and the first thing you want to do is get started with question 1. DON'T! Force yourself to overview the entire examination. It's not time wasted. A complete preview starts you off in the right direction. It provides you with key information on: exam-level of difficulty, complexity, scope and coverage areas. Once you've determined those things, you can gear up mentally. An exam scan doesn't imply a complete and thorough reading of each question. It's simply a casual, cursory, superficial examination of the entire test. Flip through the pages, and casually glance at the questions. Stop at questions that draw your interest and read them in detail.

Once you've completed the preview, you know what to expect. From that point on, your subconscious mind is working on those questions you read during the overview, while your conscious mind is concentrating on the question you're actually solving at present. Keep in mind that this overview is consuming only a small portion of your total time limit (one to three minutes). Adjust your pace accordingly. Without a test overview you start lost, with it, you have a road map.

YOUR STARTING POINT

Start any place you want to. We've all been told to start at the beginning of anything. But, are we penalized if we don't start there? No! Begin with the questions you feel most comfortable with, assuming of course, you are permitted to. Some tests are sectionalized: they group the related questions together. On these tests, if you have more knowledge in a particular area, start there. Build up your confidence early for those more difficult questions later. However, here is a word of caution--if you decide to take this approach; double check where you place your responses. Placing the response for question 46 in the response area for question 47 will foul up all questions after that point, until you discover and correct it. Correction takes valuable time. This approach is a useful one if you test in a subject that you have strong and weak areas in.

READ QUESTIONS CAREFULLY

Every question on a test contains key words, phrases and terms. If you miss or overlook these, you'll likely miss the question. Read EVERY word of a question. Hasty reading will cost you points. As you read, locate the key terms. Underline them, if you're permitted to mark in the test booklet. They are usually near the end of the question. Look for them. After reading, try to anticipate the answer, but don't misinterpret the question. Now read ALL the alternatives. Read every word of each alternative. Instead of jumping to a conclusion, temporarily delay answering until you have related the question stem to each choice and each choice to the other choices.

If you still consider your first choice the best choice, mark it. Usually first impressions are correct ones, so stick with it unless the comparison exercise above reveals something you hadn't considered previously. Remember, take one question at a time. While you're working on a question, mentally block out all other questions. Think of a hundred-question test as one hundred separate tests.

5

KEY WORDS AND PHRASES

ABSOLUTES

Key terms are the meat of a question. They may take the form of key words or key phrases. They're found in both the question stem and in the alternatives. Identify and consider them when answering a question and you won't have a problem. Overlook or ignore them, and you're in trouble. They are the essence of the statement.

Key terms are roughly equivalent to verbs in importance. The verb in a sentence is the action word that describes what is occurring. Without it the sentence has no meaning. In test taking, the key term is that critical cue to guide your thinking and treatment of the phrase or statement. Key terms describe the limit to be taken into account when considering the statement. They also indicate the degree of qualification to keep in mind when examining the phrase, or they provide the determining factor to pay attention to when inspecting a statement.

The most restrictive of the key terms is the absolutes. Watch carefully for words like:

ALWAYS	NEVER
ABSOLUTELY	ONLY
MUST	ALL
CONSTANTLY	NONE
SOLE	EVERY
NECESSARY	INVARIABLY

These words, and others, severely limit the statement they're used in. They give the phrase a note of finality. Failure to spot them will usually lead you to mark an opposite and incorrect choice.

QUALIFIERS

The second category of key terms is the qualifiers. Rather than restrict, they define, alter or modify the statement they're in. Statements containing these specifying words are mostly true. Here are a few of the more common ones:

after	frequently	more
average	generally	most
best	greatest	often
but	highest	or
chiefly	in general	partly
coincide	last	perhaps
could	later	probably
during	least	rarely
easiest	lowest	seldom
eventually	mainly	smallest
exactly	maximum	sometimes
except	may	tallest
first	minimum	usually

These words in a statement, usually provide sufficient qualifications to make it correct. This isn't always true however, so be cautious.

DETERMINERS

Unlike absolutes and qualifiers, determiners are phrases that give the statement or alternative a certain perspective. A specific mental viewpoint or relationship is presented when they're used. Some of these are:

              as judged by   you should
              on the average   most likely
              most nearly   the correct approach
              was based on   was responsible for
              most important   only part
              compared with   arising out of
              probably because   generally caused by
              depended upon   as the result of
              caused by   main advantage
              grew out of   consists of
              decreased by   probable cause

A point of reference is established when these phrases are included in a statement. Concentrate on the perspective presented when you evaluate them.

FOREIGN AND STRANGE WORDS

Test makers can generally come up with three plausible options for a question. But for some unknown reason they feel they must have four. The fourth alterntive sometimes contains a strange or foreign word or phrase. Some you could see on tests are:

              STRANGE   FOREIGN

              canniken   edelweiss
              flummex   Kadai
              hyoid   Marchesa
              caoutchouc   tarantass
              inspissate   rasbora

These words in technical or foreign language tests may be legitimate; on general tests, treat them as distractors. They make one less option to consider.

KEY WORD PERCENTAGES

*In a classic study of many classroom (teacher-made) tests, Herbert E. Hawkes, E. F. Lindquist, and C. R. Mann pointed out:

> Four out of five statements containing "all" were false;
> Four out of five statements containing "none" were true;
> Nine out of ten statements containing "only" were false;
> Three out of four statements containing "generally" were true;
> Four out of five "enumeration" statements were true;
> Two out of three "reason" or "because" statements were false;
> Three out of four statements containing "always" were false;
> The longer the statement, the more likely it is to be true.

You're now in the testing session. This is where you put it all together. In addition to the general principles mentioned earlier, there are also specific question strategies. These techniques will help you deal with individual test questions. Don't underestimate their importance. The strategies and principles used together are an unbeatable combination.

---

*From the book, THE COMPLETE GUIDE TO TAKING TESTS, by Bernard Feder. ©1979 by Bernard Feder. Published by Prentice-Hall, Inc., Englewood Cliffs, New Jersey 07632. Reproduced by permission.

6
EXAMINATION STRATEGIES

FREQUENCY OF OCCURRENCE

This type of question on CLEP tests stumped me until I discovered a system to solve it. Briefly glance at the example below, and return to the explanation. Use the following strategy on questions with compound alternatives. The answer can usually be arrived at WITHOUT knowing anything about the question. To solve it, just count the number of times each individual word or phrase appears among <u>all</u> options. Do that now. The correct answer <u>is</u> the option that has the two words that appear most often.

The following languages are spoken in the Comora Islands:

a. Spanish and Arabic
b. Arabic and French
c. German and Italian
d. French and English

Hopefully you selected option (b). The reason this strategy works is because of the nature of the question. The test maker wants to insure that you know both languages, not just one. If the correct languages appeared only once, they would

31

be paired together as one option. A person aware of only one option could correctly answer without complete knowledge. The test maker prevents this by listing half of the correct choice with an incorrect one in other alternatives. Try it again.

The elements of Ohm's law are: voltage,

a. capacitance and current
b. resistance and power
c. inductance and frequency
d. current and resistance

This strategy can be used on questions with three elements in each alternative, and also on questions with five alternatives. Although, with these two types, the answer can't always be determined with the same absolute certainty. However, you can eliminate some of the distractors which appear in different options. That will narrow your choices significantly.

LONGEST ANSWER

This strategy was briefly mentioned earlier. More should be said about the longest answer. Distractors (untrue statements) can be stated in a few words. Most test makers don't spend sufficient time composing distractors, because the correct answer is their main concern. Along with concentrating their major effort on the answer, the answer also has to be qualified, comprehensive and embracing. The results: the keyed response is usually longer than the distractors. This fact is useful if you aren't sure of the correct answer. When uncertain, go with the longest answer and you'll answer more questions correctly, than not.

Life insurance, as a method of saving:

a. is the best financial approach
b. is inferior to other plans
c. would provide less death protection
d. could be superior to other methods, depending on the person's objectives

Transactional Analysis is a way of:

a. achieving meditation
b. identifying basic communication patterns
c. bridging the subconscious
d. exercising the mind

A/AN CONNECTION

There are certain words "an" precedes and other words that "a" precedes. Words beginning with a vowel sound are usually preceded by the word "an." Example: an apple, an exit, an honor. The words honest and hour are included in this group because they start with a vowel sound, eventhough their first letter isn't a vowel. Words beginning with a non-vowel sound (consonants usually) are preceded by the word "a." Example: A woman, a name, a patch. Surprisingly, uniform, union and united are in this group.

You'll find this grammatical mistake primarily on teacher-made tests. In haste or oversight, the test maker will include distractors that aren't grammatically correct with the question stem. Transform this careless mistake into a bonus for you.

A word used in the predicate following a factitive verb to modify its direct object is an:

a. objective complement
b. nonrestrictive clause
c. parenthetical element
d. split infinitive

In geology, a glacial bowl eroded out of a lake is called a:

a. estuary
b. ostium
c. cirque
d. magnet

ROOT AND PREFIX CLUES

The majority of our words came from the Latin and Greek languages. By learning an increasing number of these root words and prefixes, you'll be better prepared to test in most subjects. Knowing the root or prefix will enable you to glean at least a partial meaning from an unfamiliar word. Complete word understanding isn't necessary; a hint is all that's needed sometimes to answer a question. The bibliography mentions some books containing excellent sections on roots and prefixes. In your spare time, learn more of these and you'll raise you score even more.

Cuprous metal would appear:

a. bronze-like
b. gold-like
c. silver-like
d. copper-like

When measuring with a nephoscope, you would be mainly concerned with:

a. heat transfer
b. sugar level
c. clouds height
d. brain waves

PHYSICAL POSITION

The physical position of an alternative can many times reveal its importance. I suggest using this strategy only if you're not certain of the answer. Traditionally, the test-option positions are standardized. Meaning, the correct answer will be in the (c) position or (b) position more often than the other two locations. There's a good reason for this. If alternative (a) was correct too frequently, most persons would select it without reading the other options. Test makers also tend to shy away from the extreme options (a) and (d). Test construction specialists want you to hunt for it, and the best way is to bury it between (a) and (d). Therefore, if you're unsure of the answer, choose either (c) or (b), in that order. Chances are, the option probabilities will produce more correct guesses.

NEGATIVE QUESTIONS

Persons unskilled in testing almost always get confused with negative questions. In "fair" questions, the negative word will be underlined, capitalized or typed in italics. Once you discover this type of question, apply the strategy. Since the negative word effectively reverses the meaning, read the statement as a positive one by OMITTING the negative word. Now you have a straight-forward statement. Because you changed the stem, you'll have to alter how you answer the alternatives. Instead of answering "yes" to the correct option, you now answer "no" to the keyed response. It takes some practice, but this strategy will unconfuse the question.

Which city is NOT in the Eastern time zone?

a. Atlanta
b. New York
c. Chicago
d. Boston

All of the following are American cars EXCEPT:

a. Mercury
b. Plymouth
c. Oldsmobile
d. Fiat

QUESTION AND ANSWER ASSOCIATION

Here is one of those sometimes unavoidable situations for the test makers. They determine that certain subject matter should be tested, however, it is almost impossible to word the stem without giving away the answer. A sincere attempt is made to phrase the stem in such a way as to not reveal the keyed response. In certain cases, however, this isn't possible. Your knowledge of common synonyms (words that mean basically the same) can greatly simplify these questions. Here are some common examples:

        athletic = muscular
        wisdom = knowledge
        detriment = harm
        legend = myth
        banquet = feast
        humane = kind

I've seen extreme cases where the answer actually restates the word in the stem. Once you've discovered the synonym, the decision-making for you is over.

    In reading development, fixations are directly related to:

    a.   comprehension
    b.   perception
    c.   speed
    d.   focusing

As applied to nonverbals, the public sphere is:

    a.   nonpersonal interaction
    b.   the business bubble
    c.   unknown to close friends
    d.   beyond your control

RELATED QUESTION DISCLOSURE

    Constructing a test is a difficult chore. The problem is complicated even more because of the total number of questions. Thinking up one hundred questions on a subject is hard enough, much less attempting to cross-reference them. Even standardized exams occasionally have an unintentional disclosure by a related question.

16. The flower girl in Harold Brighouse's "Maid of France" was:

   a. Paula
   b. Blanche
   c. Cathleen
   d. Anna

Later you read this question:

73. The author of "Maid of France" is:

   a. Dunsany
   b. Brooks
   c. Brighouse
   d. Dowson

You may not know the answer to question 16, but question 73 was answered for you.

Spykman's "Rimland Theory" maintained that the most effective means of achieving global power was:

   a. control of the seas
   b. containment
   c. political control
   d. economic action

Then you see:

Spykman's geopolitical theory placed major emphasis on:

   a. air power
   b. the rimland
   c. seapower
   d. the heartland

Occasionally, the "answer" question will appear before the related test item that asks the question. When this happens, just note the question number and locate the other question after you've completed one sweep through the test. To stop and locate the related question in the middle of the answering process will waste precious time.

ALL OF THE ABOVE

The frequency of this kind of question has diminished on standardized tests. I still however find them on many teacher-made tests. A question with an "all of the above" alternative is essentially a true-false test item. The answer can only be one of two sets of alternatives. Either "all of the above" is correct, or ONE of the other three options. Think about it. Your choice is only between "all of the above" or one other alternative. Being a true-false question, one of two conditions will exist. Either "all of the above" is correct, or it's not. Since "all of the above" alternatives are correct more often, let's solve that type first. When you suspect that "all of the above" is the correct answer, try to identify two of the other options as being correct also. Once you've confirmed those, your search is over. Using the example below: options (a) and (c) are both correct answers to the question, so neither can be the "most correct answer." Therefore, it's choice (d), the all encompassing statement. Don't even concern yourself with option (b). Once you've determined at least two choices are correct, you have the answer.

Which of the following are parts of a suit of armor?

a. breastplate
b. goget
c. visor
d. all of the above

Now, let's discuss questions when "all of the above" isn't the correct answer. Your approach here is to initially identify a distractor. Once you've found the distractor, you can eliminate it and "all of the above" from further consideration. If one of the options is incorrect, "all of the above" is also incorrect. You're now left with two choices. Take your pick. Just by locating one distractor, you've reduced the odds by one half, and increased your chances of correctly answering the question from 25% to 50%.

> In the basic communicative process, feedback is of prime importance to:
>
> a. the sender
> b. the receiver
> c. the symbols
> d. all of the above

The key word here is "prime."

NONE OF THE ABOVE

This question is basically a variation of an "all of the above" type. I can't see the logic behind a question with "none of the above" being the correct answer. It's not directly testing your knowledge of the subject, but indirectly, your ability to identify facts that aren't incorporated in the concept or principle mentioned. The "none of the above" question is also, in essence, a true-false question. The answer must be either "none of the above" or ONE of the other three options. To decide which of these is the correct answer, try to locate a choice that's true. If you can locate it, you have the correct answer. There is no need to go any further.

> Which of the following training aids could be used effectively to teach the blind?
>
> a. tape recorder
> b. 35 mm slides
> c. chalkboard
> d. none of the above

On test items that "none of the above" is correct, all you can do is attempt to confirm that the other three choices are not true, and mark "none of the above." There are no shortcuts here.

An automobile engine is mechanically attached to:

a. the gas tank
b. the battery
c. the shock absorber
d. none of the above

RELATIVE POSITION

The relative position of an alternative can provide clues to its correctness. Options are normally placed in ascending or descending order of magnitude. Numbers or qualities either go from low to high or from high to low, within the group of options. Traditional test construction recommends enclosing the correct answer within distractors of higher and lower values. This typical ranking is many times an indication that the correct answer isn't the highest or lowest value, but one in between. Use this fact to your advantage. On uncertain questions give primary consideration to the in-between options. Of course if you're sure of the answer after reading the question, don't use this strategy. But if this strategy is necessary, it will leave you two less alternatives to consider.

Carson City, Nevada is the smallest U. S. state capitol. It has a population of approximately:

a. 5,000
b. 16,000
c. 31,000
d. 48,000

What percentage of imported zinc does America depend upon to meet its consumption requirements?

a. 34%
b. 93%
c. 51%
d. 75%

You sometimes see these questions with the alternatives not in their relative positions. Simply unscramble them by listing the values or amounts in their correct order, and then use the strategy.

NONPARALLEL OPTIONS

The alternatives in a question should be equal or alike. They should express the same type of thought, quality or quantity. Options should be in the same category or class. You can't compare apples with oranges,, using the same standard of measurement. That's what a nonparallel question is asking you to do. You'll normally find them on a test because the test maker didn't put sufficient thought into devising plausible distractors. Their presence should tell you to eliminate them from consideration.

A highly systematic method of treating problems by the use of algebraic notations describes:

a. algebra
b. calculus
c. addition
d. geometry

Identifying nonparallel options won't necessarily provide you with the answer, but this approach allows you to eliminate distractors. The more alternatives you can discard, the closer you are to the answer.

Which of the following is found both in marine and fresh water?

a. mackerel
b. porpoise
c. salmon
d. perch

DOUBLE NEGATIVES

You'll rarely see a double negative question on a test. They are just as confusing to the test makers as they are to the test takers. If I had to give an example of a trick question, this would be it. Look at the example below, and see why. Without a definite strategy, the more you read it, the more confusing it becomes. To clear up a double negative question, eliminate both negative words, which changes it to a positive statement. Now read it.

Which is not something a wise test taker wouldn't do?

a. not change answers after rereading
b. change answers after rereading
c. not answer uncertain questions
d. be the first to leave the room

Two negative terms in a sentence neutralize each other, so consider it a positive statement.

"X" SUBSTITUTION

Math problems are difficult for most individuals. When the unknown factor "x" is present, the level of difficulty increases. Substituting a known number or amount can greatly simplify solving it. When you substitute, just select a number. Make it easier for yourself and choose a simple number. Replace the unknown with your selected number and solve the problem. After solving it, convert the answer back to the "x" format or use it to determine the correct option. This system really simplifies the problem solving steps.

While shopping at the supermarket you purchase, among other things, a can of cherries at a cost of "x" cents. The jar of dressing you selected is priced at 2x cents. The cigarettes were priced at 3 times the cost of the dressing. What is the difference in cost, between the cherries and the cigarettes?

a. 4x
b. 4x + 3
c. 5x
d. 5x + 5

A word of caution: you can only use this substitution method on items containing "multiple" elements exclusively. In the example above the element values were x, 2x, and 6x. Once a variable such as 2x + 10 is introduced in the question, substituting isn't a foolproof approach.

JUDGMENT QUESTIONS

There are factual questions and there are judgment questions. Factual questions can be answered with a definite yes or no: true or false. Judgment questions are different. There may not be a definite, supportable answer to it--but a standard is used. The answer is the choice that knowledgable, capable and experienced individuals agree the answer to be. There is a general consensus among them as to the preferable answer. To answer judgment questions, you must think like the test maker thinks and use common sense. Disregard your preferences and opinions, and mark "the book" answer. During a test is the wrong time to voice your disagreement or answer "in spite." Your score will reflect this damaging act of defiance. Answer it as the experts agree it should be answered and you'll be points ahead.

A serious acccident occurs five-hundred yards in front of you. As a driver you should:

a. continue driving
b. stop and help
c. say a prayer
d. drive more carefully

Your goal in presenting a technical briefing is to:

a. state a position
b. indicate its shortcomings
c. provide your opinion
d. present the facts

DECEPTIVE COMPUTATION

Whenever you see a math question, you assume some computation is required. For deceptive computation-type questions, that's what the test maker wants you to think. These questions, at first glance, appear to require the use of higher math to solve them: but not so. The long and complicated stem is designed to give you that impression. When you're presented with a math type question-- stop and determine what it's asking for. Ignore the unessentials. Forget the parts that don't directly relate to solving the problem. Most deceptive computation questions can be solved by logical reasoning, without the use of any complicated computation.

Compute the area of this circle with a 45° sector area of 13 square inches.

a. 78
b. 104
c. 127
d. 131

Try and figure out the above question before you continue reading. Let's use the strategy. If you look carefully at the circle you can see the sector (slice) is a definite portion of the complete circle. How many of these sectors make up the circle? Mentally double the slice and you'll see that two sectors are 1/4 of the circle. If two sectors are 1/4 a circle, then one sector is 1/8 of a circle. Multiply the sector area by 8 and you'll have the answer. Common sense, logical reasoning and careful observation are all that are needed for deceptive-computation type questions.

You determine your monthly car operating cost to be $75.00 for every 1,000 miles driven. Last month you drove 2,300 miles. Your operating cost was:

a. $152.50
b. $172.50
c. $142.50
d. $92.50

A careful look at both the figures in the stem and in the alternatives will put you on the right track. Last month's mileage was more than twice the 1,000 mile standard. All alternatives less than twice $75.00 are distractors. With two choices left, common sense tells you $152.50 is too close to $150.00, considering last month's mileage was 300 miles over your 2,000 mile reference. You have the answer. You can save time on many math questions by carefully analyzing them and taking a simple approach.

COMPLEX QUESTIONS

Have you ever read a question that gave you a headache? I have, and it was a complex question. They appear to be the most difficult questions on a test. Don't let their perplexing stem and multitude of options trick you into believing that they're more difficult than any other question. They aren't: in fact, some are easier. An effective plan of action is all you need to solve these. Look at the question below and refer to the explanation following it.

As a home health aide, you are serving a patient her meal. In which order should the following steps be accomplished? (1) provide eating utensils; (2) wash your hands; (3) dispose of leftovers; (4) prepare food; (5) serve food.

a. 4, 2, 1, 4, 3
b. 2, 1, 5, 3, 4
c. 4, 2, 1, 5, 3
d. 2, 4, 1, 5, 3

Since the first number in all options is either 2 or 4, first determine which is the first step. Follow the same procedure with the last numbers 3 and 4. Then locate the alternative that has the first and last number in the correct slot and that's the answer. If two options have the first and last step correct, study the internal steps and determine, using logical reasoning, the proper sequence. Just by identifying the first and last steps you can usually eliminate half the alternatives. Knowing all the steps isn't necessary. Partial knowledge and common sense is all you need.

You decide to fix that leaky faucet. With all parts and tools available, which sequence should you use to repair it? (1) separate stem and packing nut; (2) put it back together; (3) remove stem and packing nut; (4) shut off water; (5) remove faucet handle.

a. 5, 4, 3, 1, 2
b. 4, 1, 5, 2, 3
c. 4, 5, 3, 1, 2
d. 5, 2, 4, 3, 1

In addition to the above type of complex question, there is another kind. The previous type simply requested the proper sequence. For this next type, you have to pick items from a list that apply to the question. The prime skill you'll use here is the process of elimination.

Cost is an important consideration in purchasing a home. The price of a home is primarily determined by these: (1) improvements; (2) real estate agent; (3) neighborhood; (4) air rights; (5) zoning; (6) square footage

a. 1, 3, 4 and 6 only
b. 2, 4, 5 and 6 only
c. 1, 2, 4 and 5 only
d. 1, 3, 5 and 6 only
e. 2, 3, 4 and 6 only

There are a number of ways to approach this problem. Process of elimination is perhaps the fastest way. Identify one element that normally WOULD NOT affect the price, and eliminate the choices containing that element. That leaves you with two or three remaining. Attempt to identify another distractor, and eliminate those choices. The remaining choice is the correct answer.

INCONSISTENT FORM

Grammatical cues make this strategy possible. All choices in a question should be grammatically correct with their stem. When they aren't, the complete statement (stem and alternative) doesn't sound right when you read it. It's important to "read through" the stem, attaching each choice to it, to form a complete sentence. This requires you to read the stem four times on a four alternative question. When doing this, if an alternative doesn't sound correct, or isn't consistent with the other options, it probably isn't the answer. Eliminate the inconsistent choices, and you're left with fewer to select from, or the correct answer.

Federal education grants were started by President Kennedy. The basic purpose of a grant is:

a. supplementing college cost
b. to help the needy student
c. to award academic excellence
d. achieve high grades

To be a "drug on the market" is:

a. consuming over-the-counter prescriptions
b. taking illegal substances
c. dealing in drugs
d. to be excess to demands or needs

SIMILAR CHOICES

Certain questions you'll encounter have options that are closely related or almost identical. This should be your clue to apply the similar-choice strategy. Just by identifying this type of question, you've reduced it from a multiple choice item to basically a true and false statement. The similar choices cannot BOTH be correct, as you must select the MOST correct answer. If both related options are equal in completeness and scope, the answer has to be an option other than the related ones.

A synonym for the word bequem is:

a. hazard
b. risk
c. comfortable
d. danger

A quenella is a:

a. doughnut
b. garnish
c. cake
d. tart

Another situation could, however, be present. One option may be more encompassing and inclusive than the other similar option. When this is present, the answer is either the option of greater scope, or the opposite choice. This process of elimination will reduce the alternatives to a more manageable number.

Yttrium is a type of:

a.   metal
b.   magnesium
c.   nickel
d.   gas

OPPOSITE CHOICES

A close relative of the similar choice question is the opposite choice item. The difference here is that the options oppose each other. The usual opposite-choice question will have two options saying almost the same thing, and the other two options stating a conflicting viewpoint. Your initial decision isn't to decide which of the four choices is correct; first determine which of the two differing viewpoints is accurate. Then select the more encompassing and complete option of the two. If both choices are equal in scope, and you don't know which is correct, take a wild guess.

In business, the victim of a "bait and switch" scheme is the:

a.   customer
b.   merchant
c.   retailer
d.   woman

A variation of the above question is one containing the options "all of the above" or "none of the above." If "all of the above" is an option, it must be a distractor. The alternatives that express opposing viewpoints can't BOTH be correct, therefore "all of the above" is automatically eliminated. Questions with "none of the above" aren't as simple to evaluate. Normally "none of the above" is also a distractor. If it's the correct answer, very little is gained from the question. The only purpose it could serve is to test your ability to identify incorrect options, while never determining whether you actually know the answer. So proceed with caution.

A source of income for the federal government is corporate and personal income taxes. In perspective, corporate and personal tax rates:

    a.   vary in many aspects
    b.   are identical
    c.   share a common tax schedule
    d.   none of the above

OVERLAPPING ALTERNATIVES

Earlier I discussed the most encompassing, most comprehensive, and the most inclusive answer. The overlapping alternatives strategy is fundamentally that approach. This technique can be applied to the following question.

We communicate in numerous ways. Listening constitutes what percentage of our average communicating day?

    a.   less than 30%
    b.   less than 40%
    c.   more than 50%
    d.   more than 60%

Notice how the two sets of alternatives overlap each other. If (a) is true, then (b) must also be true. less than 30% is included in less than 40%. If (d) is correct, (c) has to be correct also. It is apparent that more than 60% is included in more than 50%. These two keen observations will allow you to quickly change a four-alternative question into a less complicated two-choice item. Since option (b) encompasses (a), and choice (c) overlaps (d), your choice is either (b) or (c).

In England and Germany, one trillion dollars is written with:

    a.   less than nine zeros
    b.   less than twelve zeros
    c.   more than fifteen zeros
    d.   more than eighteen zeros

7

AFTER THE EASY QUESTIONS

NOW THE HARD QUESTIONS

You've answered the easy questions, and by now your mental powers are at their peak. This is the best time to deal with the more difficult test items. Somewhere on your scratch paper you should have a list of these uncertain test items, along with their possible answers for reconsideration. Start at the top of the list and work down. Return to the beginning of the test and read the first unanswered question again. If you previously isolated the answer to two or three options, only consider those.

During this phase of testing, you will probably have happen to you what almost always happens to me--those hard questions suddenly become easier! I can't completely account for this sudden insight. I assume it's a combination of factors. As you progress through the test, you steadily increase your level of concentration, and your mind focuses almost exclusively on the subject. At this point, you're able to solve the more difficult questions you were unable to solve at the beginning of the test. Your subconscious mind has had a chance to sort things out and see new relationships. Exposure to all the questions gives you added perception. This insight, many times, will trigger a chain of thought leading to the answer. Take advantage of this and overwhelm those troublesome questions.

An efficient plan of attack is required. If you can't come up with the answer after reading it twice, forget that question and go to the next one. Use the same time-saving procedure as before. After you've answered all the easier ones, start at the top of your list again, and go through the remaining unanswered test items. Repeat this process a total of three times. The still unanswered questions are now classified as "chance-guess" items. All you can do is guess; so guess.

COMPUTE YOUR "ROUGH" SCORE

At the end of the session, compute your "rough" score. Count the number of questions you didn't know. Divide that number by the number of alternatives or options in one test question. The answer you arrive at is the approximate number of "uncertain" or "guessed-at" questions you statistically answered correctly. Add that figure to the number of questions you answered the first time through, and you have your "rough" test score. Remember it, and compare it with the actual score you receive. I've had much success calculating my scores this way, and I'm sure you'll experience the same success. This method doesn't consider certain variables, as I feel they cancel each other out.

A RESPONSE FOR EVERY QUESTION

To insure there aren't any unmarked test items, you should perform a response count. Since you can't be sure by just glancing at the answer sheet, a full count is necessary. But don't start with question 1. If you do, and get distracted during the count, the tendency is to resume counting at the location you thought you left off at. That may not be true, as you could've missed a response. Therefore, begin counting at some unconventional place. Question 100 or at the top of a column is a convenient starting point. If you discover an unanswered question, locate it in the test book to determine where you went wrong. Also check the question preceding it to verify its correctness. There could be a possibility of an earlier error, creating a series of wrong responses. If this did happen, you must go back every five questions until you locate the origin of your error. The response check is an excellent way to insure a response for every question.

CHECK FOR MISMARKS

You now know that all the desired marks are on the answer sheet, but you don't know if they're in the correct places. In the remaining time, accomplish a response verification. This step is not intended as a double-check on your choice of answers. This isn't the time to change answers. It's designed to verify that you responded the way you intended to. An error, such as marking (d) for (b), will cost you points. A response verification is designed to locate and correct this mistake. Start at question 1, and continue from there. Read each question stem and identify the option you previously selected. Refer to the answer sheet and determine if that's the response you actually marked. The verification takes less time than you might think, and it's a worthwhile check.

DETERMINE TEST COMPOSITION

This should be the last post-test activity, if you have time left. Determining the test composition isn't a must. You decide whether you'll do it or not. I routinely do it, just to determine the emphasis placed on different sub-subject areas.

After a test in psychology, I want to know the number of questions that addressed behavior, or the percentage of human development questions on the test. My approach is to list the areas, e.g., learning, personality, deviance, etc., on my scratch paper. As I review each test question, I classify it and mark it under the various divisions I listed. After completing this exercise, I'm aware of areas of concentration and omission. I go a step further and compute the percentage each subject area consumed of the complete test. With that knowledge, I can better prepare for similar exams in the future.

8
AFTER THE TEST

TEST REVIEW

You've probably been wondering about the cassette recorder. Now is the time for it. The test should be reviewed immediately after you leave the testing room. Satisfy your physical needs first, but don't do anything else before the review. At this point in time, the test is still fresh in your mind. You can recall the vast majority of it. Your ability to recall will quickly diminish as the minutes pass. Review now!

I go directly to a quiet place and start looking through my study and reference materials. To provide a record of my review, I use a cassette recorder because I can't write fast enough. I record all the experiences I've been exposed to during the test. I verify the correct answers and my errors. This review record becomes my study reference if I ever take a similar test again. This record is a PERSONAL guide, not to be given or loaned to anyone. Serious legal and ethical problems will arise if you compromise the exam. Prevent any possible difficulty and keep it to yourself. That way, you're within your legal rights. Most individuals already review their exams, but without a definite system.

During the review or at some later date, review the review. Find out why you missed certain questions and capitalize on those mistakes in future tests. Determine your success rate on the questions you guessed at. There are many personal applications. It will be one of your most useful study references in the future.

AFTER THOUGHTS

Give yourself a pat on the back for successfully applying the guidelines, techniques and strategies of test taking. You can be confident that you'll receive the highest possible score. Mentally review the test-taking skills to identify specific areas you may need to read again for better understanding. It's never too early to prepare for your next test.

BIBLIOGRAPHY

American College, "Test Wiseness: Test-Taking Skills for Adults," McGraw-Hill, New York, 1978.

Clark, Bruce C., General (Ret), "How to Study and Take Tests," Soldiers Magazine, U. S. Army, April 1976, pp. 31-33.

Educational Testing Service, "Multiple Choice Questions: A Close Look," Educational Testing Service, Princeton, NJ, 1973.

Feder, Bernard, "How to Pass Without Actually Cheating," Human Behavior, June 1977, pp. 57-59.

Feder, Bernard, "The Complete Guide to Taking Tests," Prentice-Hall, Englewood Cliffs, NJ, 1979.

Honig, Fred, "Taking Tests and Scoring High," ARCO Publishing Co., New York, 1967.

Hook, J. N., "Testmanship - Seven Ways to Raise Your Examination Grades," Barnes & Noble, New York, 1969.

Huff, Darrell, "SCORE - The Strategy of Taking Tests," Ballantine Books, New York, 1961.

Juola, Arvo E., "Examination Skills and Techniques," Cliff's Notes, Lincoln, Nebraska, 1968.

Millman, Jason, and Walter Pauk, "How to Take Tests," McGraw-Hill, New York, 1969.

Oliver, Rose, "Overcoming Test Anxiety," reprint from Rational Living, Spring 1975.

Taylor, James S., "Improve Your Classroom Testing Skills," The Clearing House, May 1977, pp. 381-385.

University of Maryland, "Test Taking Tips," University of Maryland - European Division, Pamphlet UMED - 22, undated.